# Your Body
# Babies

*Anna Sandeman*

W
FRANKLIN WATTS
LONDON • SYDNEY

This edition published in 2000
© Aladdin Books Ltd 1996
*Designed and produced by*
**Aladdin Books Ltd**
28 Percy Street
London W1P 0LD

*First published in
Great Britain in 1990 by*
**Franklin Watts**
96 Leonard Street
London EC2A 4XD

*Design:* David West Children's Books
*Designer:* Edward Simkins
*Illustrator:* Ian Thompson
*Picture Research:* Brooks Krikler Research
*Consultants:* Dr R Levene MB.BS, DCH, DRCOG
Jan Bastoncino Dip. Ed., teacher of biology and
science to 5-12 year-olds

ISBN 0-7496-2450-7 (hardback)
ISBN 0-7496-3895-8 (paperback)

Printed in Belgium

A CIP catalogue record for this book is
available from the British Library.

Photocredits
Abbreviations: t-top, m-middle, b-bottom,
r-right, l-left
All the pictures in this book were taken by Roger
Vlitos apart from the pictures on the following pages:
6-7m: Frank Spooner Pictures; 8-9m, 12tl, 12-13m, 13,
14tl, 14-15m, 18t, 29r: Science Photo Library

# Contents

# Pregnancy

Can you remember
being a baby –
when you
couldn't walk,
talk, or even sit up?
Doesn't it seem like a long
time ago?

Most animals develop and
grow much quicker than humans. A lamb or foal
struggles to its feet minutes after it has been born.
Both are able to look after themselves within a
few weeks. A human baby will probably not
walk without help until after its first birthday
and is not expected to take care of itself for at
least 16 years.

Even before birth, a human baby takes much longer to develop than most other animal babies. A human mother is pregnant for nine months. A mouse gives birth after 20 days, a cat after nine weeks. The populations of these animals can increase quickly. Only large animals, such as the whale or the elephant, are pregnant for longer – the first for twelve months, the second for 23 months.

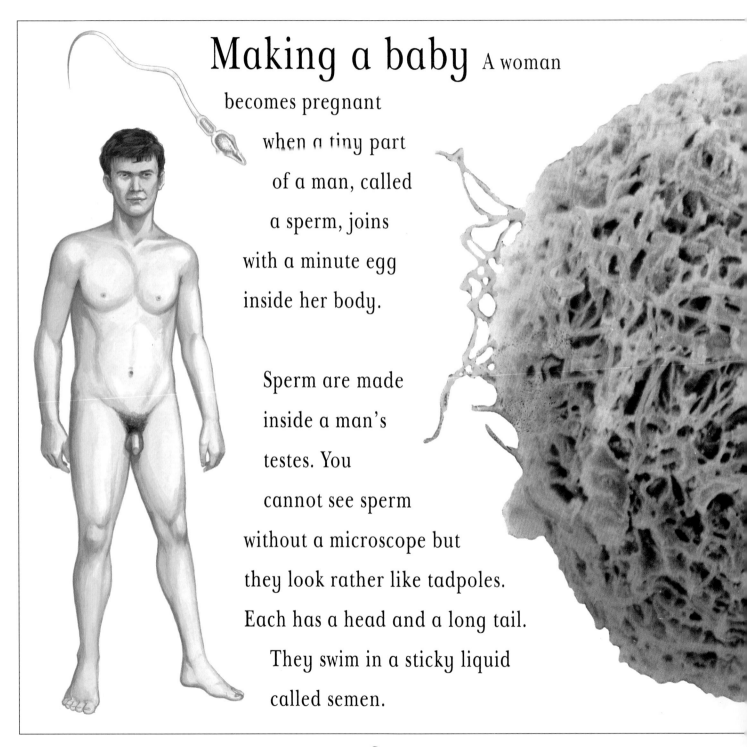

# Making a baby

A woman becomes pregnant when a tiny part of a man, called a sperm, joins with a minute egg inside her body.

Sperm are made inside a man's testes. You cannot see sperm without a microscope but they look rather like tadpoles. Each has a head and a long tail. They swim in a sticky liquid called semen.

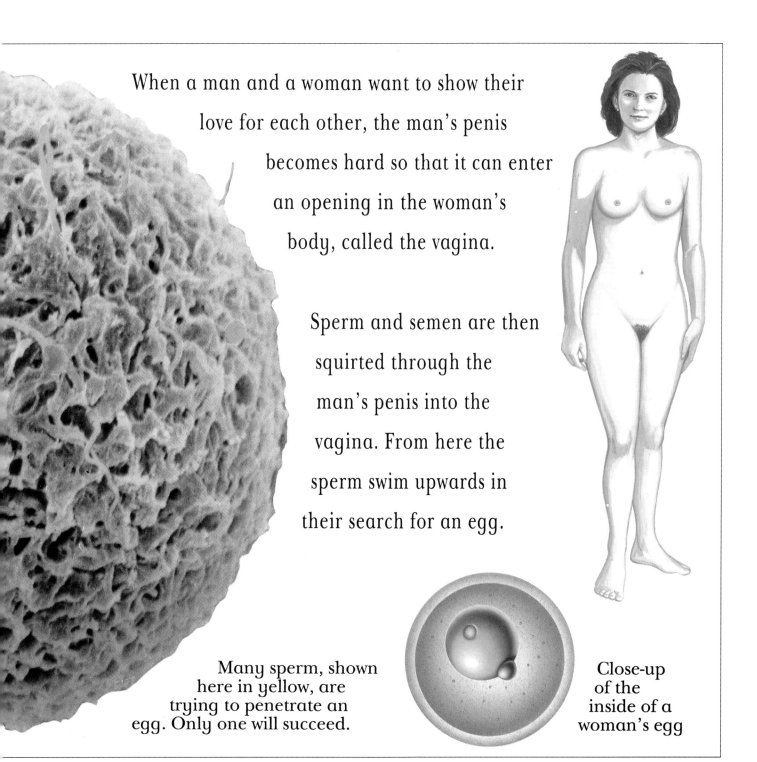

When a man and a woman want to show their love for each other, the man's penis becomes hard so that it can enter an opening in the woman's body, called the vagina.

Sperm and semen are then squirted through the man's penis into the vagina. From here the sperm swim upwards in their search for an egg.

Many sperm, shown here in yellow, are trying to penetrate an egg. Only one will succeed.

Close-up of the inside of a woman's egg

A fertilised egg divides to form one baby.

# One baby or two?
A woman's eggs are stored in her ovaries.

Every month an egg leaves an ovary to travel down one of two fallopian tubes leading to the uterus. If it meets and joins with a sperm, the egg is fertilised. The fertilised egg is now an embryo. This is the beginning of the baby which will be born nine months later.

A fertilised egg splits into two cells. These two cells divide again and again to form a ball of cells. The ball of cells travels on to the uterus where it settles into the soft lining.

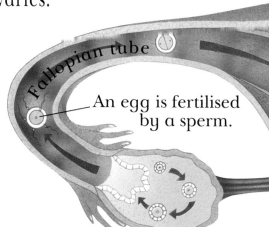

Fallopian tube

An egg is fertilised by a sperm.

Ovary

The embryo embeds.

Vagina

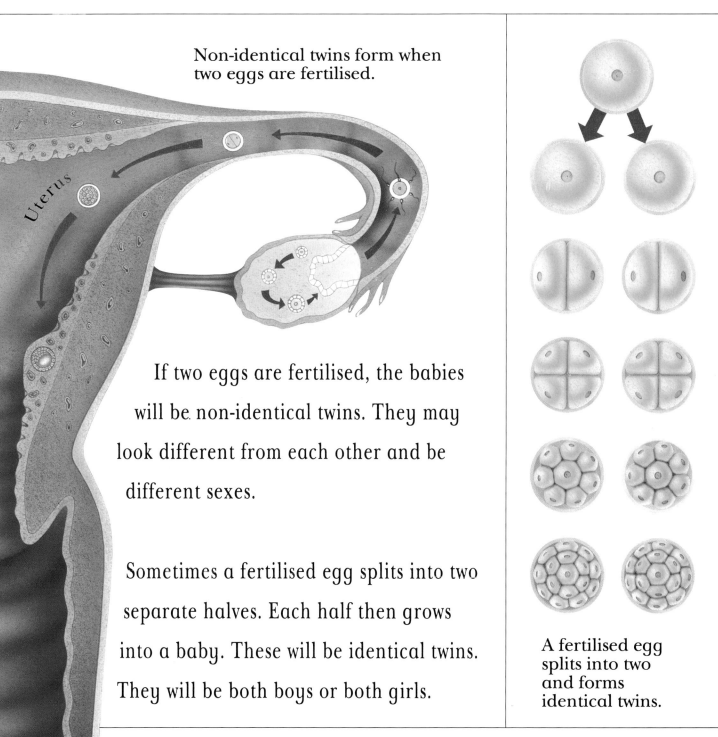

Non-identical twins form when two eggs are fertilised.

Uterus

If two eggs are fertilised, the babies will be non-identical twins. They may look different from each other and be different sexes.

Sometimes a fertilised egg splits into two separate halves. Each half then grows into a baby. These will be identical twins. They will be both boys or both girls.

A fertilised egg splits into two and forms identical twins.

# Starting to grow

**An embryo at 30 days**

Inside the uterus, the cells grow rapidly. They quickly begin to take the shape of a head and backbone.

By day 25 the heart is beating, even though the baby is only small – about the size of a baked bean.

By week eight, the baby is 25 millimetres long. Although it is small it already has arms and legs, fingers and toes. It also has the beginnings of a mouth and a nose.

An embryo at eight weeks

The baby lives inside a kind of bag filled with liquid. This protects the baby against any bumps and stops the baby becoming too hot or too cold.

The baby is fed by its mother. The food comes in tiny particles, called nutrients. These pass from the mother's blood into a tube, called the umbilical cord, and then into the baby. Look at your tummy button and you will see where your umbilical cord once grew. After birth, the baby no longer needs its umbilical cord so it dries up and drops off.

An embryo at eleven weeks

# Getting bigger

At 16 weeks the baby is about 13 centimetres long and weighs less than 100 grammes. It has developed eyes, ears, a nose and a mouth as well as finger and toe nails. At this stage the baby grows quickly and the mother's tummy is getting larger.

An embryo at 20 weeks

The embryo at 16 weeks is developing rapidly.

At 20 weeks the mother can feel the baby kicking as it grows and its muscles get stronger. The baby can hear, swallow and suck its thumb. It is beginning to recognise its mother's voice. Some babies even get hiccups!

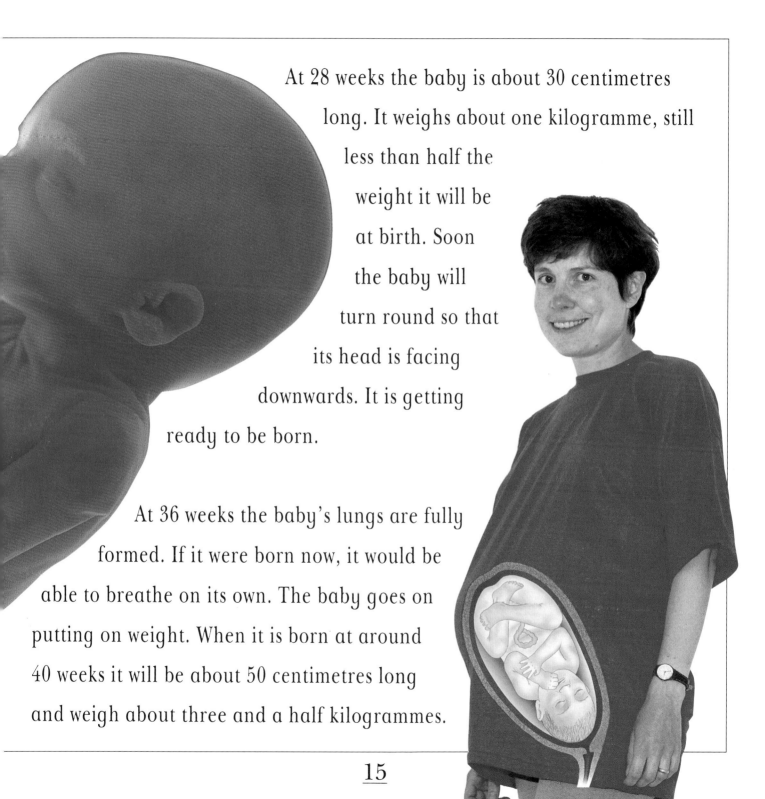

At 28 weeks the baby is about 30 centimetres long. It weighs about one kilogramme, still less than half the weight it will be at birth. Soon the baby will turn round so that its head is facing downwards. It is getting ready to be born.

At 36 weeks the baby's lungs are fully formed. If it were born now, it would be able to breathe on its own. The baby goes on putting on weight. When it is born at around 40 weeks it will be about 50 centimetres long and weigh about three and a half kilogrammes.

# Family likeness

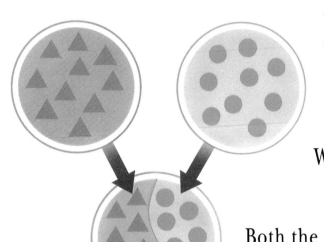

When a baby is born, friends and relatives often say that it looks like its mum or dad. Why?

Both the sperm from the dad, and the egg from the mum, which join up to start a baby, carry their own kind of body pattern. When the egg is fertilised, the two patterns mix together to make a new pattern. This new pattern becomes the body plan for the baby.

Look at this photo of an eight year-old and his parents. Who does the boy look more like?

The patterns that a mother and father pass on to their baby are made up of the patterns given to them by their own parents. This means that a baby may also look a little like its grandparents.

Ask if you can use photos of your family to make a family tree. Look at eyes, noses and mouths to see which are most like yours. Look at your brothers and sisters too. How are they like you?

# Newborn baby

A baby grows most quickly before it is born. After birth, growth is slower. By the end of its first year, it is about three times its birth weight.

As a baby grows, it changes shape. A newborn baby looks very different from you. Although its head is big – about a quarter of the length of its body – its arms reach down only to its hips. Measure the length of your head and arms compared with the rest of you.

Four months

One year

Three years

Look at the pictures below to see how a child's body changes between birth and the age of twelve. What do you notice?

Six years

Ten years

Twelve years

# Muscles

Unlike most animals, a newborn baby is almost completely helpless. It can't walk, talk, sit or even lift its head. Its muscles are too weak. Almost all it can do is cry – very loudly.

But from the moment of birth, a baby starts exercising. It waves its arms about and kicks its legs to make its muscles stronger. At this stage, the baby has no control over its movements so it may hit itself in the face by mistake.

Gradually babies learn to use other muscles. By the age of three months, most babies are trying to prop themselves up on their forearms.

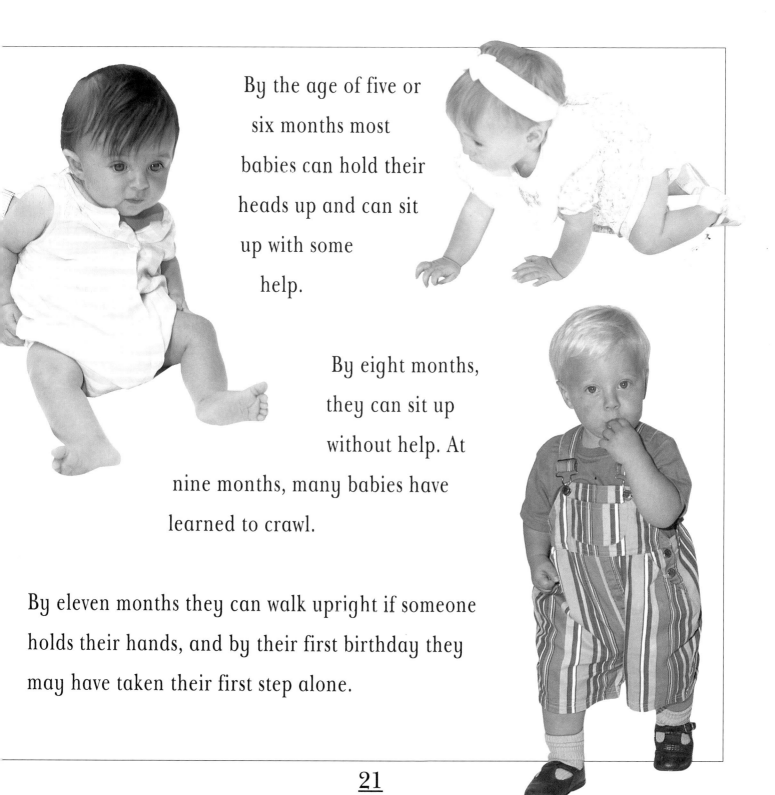

By the age of five or six months most babies can hold their heads up and can sit up with some help.

By eight months, they can sit up without help. At nine months, many babies have learned to crawl.

By eleven months they can walk upright if someone holds their hands, and by their first birthday they may have taken their first step alone.

# Senses
Although newborn babies can't move much, they can see, hear, taste, smell and feel things around them.

At first babies can only clearly see things which are very close. When a baby is four weeks old, it watches its mother's face closely as she speaks.

Even very young babies are startled by sudden loud noises. They may blink, cry, fling their arms up, or lie quiet.

Babies are soothed by soft rhythmic sounds. Lullabies, or even a clock ticking may send them to sleep.

Babies have a strong sense of taste and can suck very hard. At first they live just on milk, which they suck from their mother or from a feeding bottle. When they are between three and six months old, they are usually given their first solid food. Most babies quickly make it clear which foods they like and which they don't.

Babies have a sense of smell, too. They even recognise their mothers by their smell.

Crying babies often calm down if they are picked up and cuddled.

# Body control

Slowly babies learn to control different parts of their body. At three months they can hold a rattle for a few seconds. At five months, they can grab a nearby toy with two hands. At six or seven months, they can feed themselves with a biscuit and help to hold a spoon while eating.

They now reach for a toy with one hand.

A month or two later, most babies can hold a toy brick in each hand. They turn the bricks around to feel their shape and enjoy banging them on the table.

At ten months, they can bring their thumb and finger together to pick up much smaller objects, such as a piece of string or a pea, and move them carefully from one place to another.

By 18 months they will usually have learned to pile bricks on top of each other or to push objects along the floor with their hands.

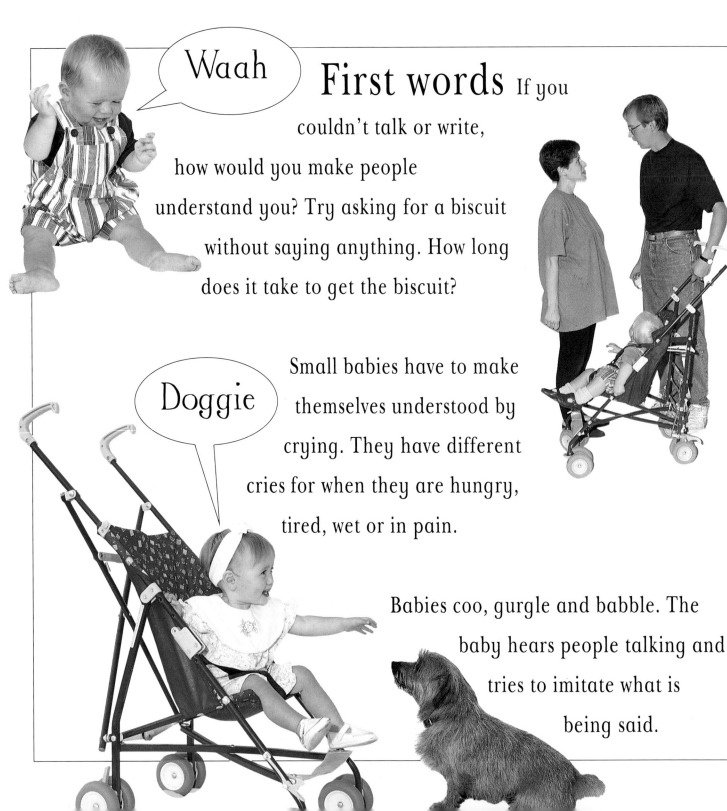

**Waah**

# First words

If you couldn't talk or write, how would you make people understand you? Try asking for a biscuit without saying anything. How long does it take to get the biscuit?

**Doggie**

Small babies have to make themselves understood by crying. They have different cries for when they are hungry, tired, wet or in pain.

Babies coo, gurgle and babble. The baby hears people talking and tries to imitate what is being said.

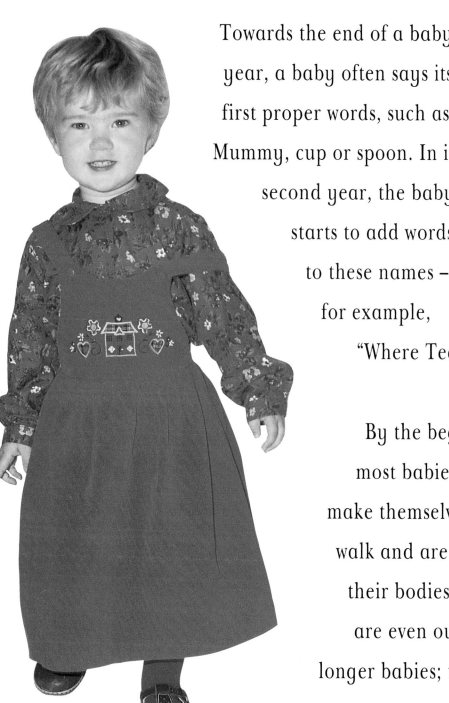

Towards the end of a baby's first year, a baby often says its first proper words, such as Mummy, cup or spoon. In its second year, the baby starts to add words to these names – for example, "Where Teddy?", "Nice doggie".

By the beginning of their third year most babies know enough words to make themselves understood. They can walk and are getting better at making their bodies do what they want. Some are even out of nappies! They are no longer babies; they have become toddlers.

# Did you know?

...that a newborn baby's brain is one quarter the weight of an adult's brain, even though an adult is twenty times heavier than a baby?

...that a woman in Russia gave birth to a total of 69 children? She had 16 pairs of twins, seven sets of triplets and four sets of quadruplets.

...that more boys are born than girls? Most babies are born between April and July.

...that if you hold a newborn baby upright, with its feet on the floor, it will try to take steps?

...that a baby has about 350 bones in its body – that's about 150 more than a grown-up?

...that a woman's egg is smaller than a full stop?

# Glossary

**Egg** – The female sex cell produced by the ovaries

**Ovaries** – The female organs that produce eggs

**Fertilisation** – The process by which a female egg and male sperm join to develop into a new baby

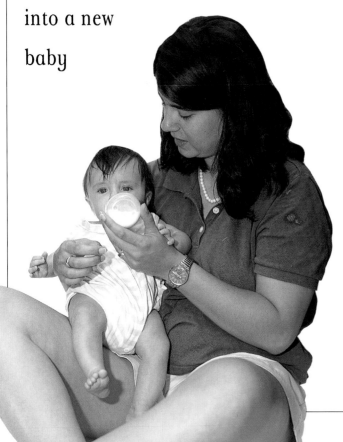

**Pregnancy** – The development of a young animal inside the uterus

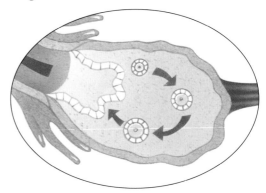

**Sperm** – The male sex cell produced by the testes

**Uterus** – The female organ in which the baby develops until it is born

# Index